WOODS RIVER ROAD

John Sewell

Fair Acre Press

First published in Great Britain in 2021 by Fair Acre Press
www.fairacrepress.co.uk

A CIP catalogue record for this book is available from the British Library

ISBN 978-1-911048-47-3

Typeset by Nadia Kingsley
Cover design by Karen Sayer
Cover image © Sara Johnson 2021

for Tess

WOODS

The hawthorn empties itself of fieldfares,
they fly like pepper dust, settle on snowfields.

A midlife traveller, I paused in the wood
too long under branches salted with berries.

JACK IN THE GREEN

I carried the mirror, an empty oblong of sky
from bedroom to wood - stood it
a tremouring pool of green, against a tree:

shyly hugging your breasts
step from the leaves
into the leaves.

*

I heard a sigh and went in deeper,
my tablespoon of blue milk
on the mossy bole:

you opened as a sunlit clearing
ramages of longings
poured out of me like leaves.

*

Such altering sweetness from the gorse
one breath and we couldn't rest
till we found the covert:

our single stripe of sunlight
on its shadows, the scent we make there
crazing grass stems, inciting leaves.

*

The lettered trunk a workmate
for my feet, the sloping bank
yeasty with ferns backs you as keenly

slides home the hasp:
a tiny gasp
fire-red as a bramble leaf.

*

Later, with much effort
we got to our feet, walked
out of the wood

stared into each other's face
brushed each other's hair
of leaves.

CELEBRATING BELTANE

Easy, sliding your dress-hem upwards, easing
each knee sideways, having them give so gently.
No accident neither, you had nothing on beneath:
posing as cellist with a cello I could see
right through; jackknifing the sofa; rolling
Kafka-esque on the hallway carpet, legs
flagging me down to end the torment - but not
just yet, not with rooms upstairs to incandesce.

We could have slept on a clothes line or the bed
of a band-saw sawing up bookshelves.

Starlings chuckled and whistled when our eyes opened
on the sunniest broadloom we'd both ever seen,
you cushioned my head - merry dancer
pulling back the clouds to dance for me.

AMPLEXUS

One hundred percent head over heels.
Next day I'm there again so full of it,
wanting to make love but the words won't join.

Our intercourse has been the poetry of my life -
thus Jefferson Hogg to Jane his wife,
once also Shelley's 'best and brightest'.
In other words, he fucked her too
and vica versa - small boat / parked car
rocking in the slow lap of the fields.

When the grip is on there's nothing else but this -
blindly, repeatedly playing the sun
to your nakedness, your half-turned neck.
The whetted word, I take it to my lips
Gentle, you whisper, *Gentle and slow.*

CHERRIES

You - spooning a mango or wiping the sex
        of a peach from your chin.
Then next day adamant that apple, no-nonsense
        apple is as far as you will go.

Things paired are things kept sweet, like governors
        on engines, the twin stalks of cherries.
I halve the bag, give you first pick. Stripping wishbone
        after wishbone, you wish my wish.

PILLOW BOOK

You laugh when I say:
And your legs stretched out
like the wings of a bird.

Like that? you ask
as we sky the meadowgrass:
'Two Swallows with a Single Heart'.

LAID PAPER

Here's a seal, a dandy-roll to this pure sheet.

You'd finished writing, went upstairs to add
a special touch, effuse a postscript just for me -
two beads of clearest lust distilled onto a page
whose bed is all imagination-stained.

Let me reciprocate with this small blob
of ruttish opaline. Too little, nothing shows.
Too much, and it dries phosphoric. Too scattered
and the wet sheet printed on its mate
will blot the splattering but leave a worn out
cockled look, which isn't what I had in mind.

This is sex by origami. Laid paper.
The brown manilla wings across my lips.
I badge it with my tongue tip and it flies.

BETWEEN ACTS

I wanted there and then to drag you into bed
the state of my knickers was evidence of that,
sorry this is rushed, I write while Bob is in the bath,
oh sod the photo album, sod seeing you happy
with someone else, last week I thought my god
if this is how it is, at my age, in a Metro
aerobics in a row boat, going at it
like there's no tomorrow (I'm sure that was a face
between the leaves), it's mad it has to end
then last night at the interval pouring coffees
and you there, preferring yours 'hot and sweet' indeed,
handing me the book, the letter wedged inside,

I couldn't wait, dashed to the Ladies, sat and read
until the curtain lifted on Act 2.

A COUPLE MAKING LOVE

It's not their bodies they're watching in the circular mirror
on the bentwood stand, her hand at the thread of weighted silk
she draws from him; his, sunning the freckles on her breast.

What they're more intent on, is their conjoined faces pooled
together, beginning to forget themselves, assume the look of lovers
making love before their eyes, oblivious to anything beyond
the other's pleasure. Voyeurs whose watchful looks come back
redoubled now the mirror's held them close, instated them as one.

THE CHAIR

In the backyard for weeks now facing the wall,
two plastic stacking chairs - a red one
mounted on a grey, their legs aligned, the seat
of one tipped forward slightly on the other.

Each time I pass I glance their way - to the fox
and vixen screaming nightly, all night, for release;
you and I in the full-height, bedroom mirror.

SWEET PEA

I would with this flower purse its four lips together
for the line of the inner lips' greater projection
        and suffusion of colour,

or gently spread them apart so the stipule inside
not pink like the lips, but a washed-through white with no scent
        to speak of, proudly stands out,

I would take each part to my mouth or simply look
and go on looking, and it wouldn't lose anything by this
        or grow ugly or commonplace

quite the reverse: forgive me, but someone as serious
about flowers, as floriferous even, should know
        and understand this perfectly.

THE TRADE

We bartered. My book of love poems
for something in her gallery.

I know, she said, unlocking a cabinet
placing her hand on a clear glass heart

cold and solid as the shaft of an icicle
when she laid it into mine.

BETRAYAL

After we fuck each other goodnight, she and I,
and fall asleep, you're there so vividly I don't know
whose limb I'm touching when I say: I love you.

So much so, that next morning when I gently
fuck her from behind, since she doesn't want to be
woken completely - neither, I realise, do I.

BOGART'S SECRET LIFE

Humphrey Bogart had a 15 year affair with Verita Thompson,
his personal assistant, known to Bogart as 'Pete'.

It turns out everything was not enough.
It could never be. Not ever. But as he said,
Who checks the facts? When they asked him: *Bogie,*
who's the broad? He'd answer: *Pete's my hairdresser*
and mistress. But keep it under wraps.
They couldn't tell a rib from what was actual.

He'd fooled Warners too. He and Pete
had been a number for two years
before that day she came to Make-up
to fit the muff to his thinning hair.
Sign her up, he said afterwards. *She'll do.*
What did you say her name was?

The next ten years were theirs - on tours, locations.
The klieg lights on the set were barely cold
before the phone was going in her suite:
Pour me a smash of loudmouth, Pete, I'm on my way.
When he proposed, she told him No,
she wanted what they had to last, and anyway

he had such lousy taste in wives.
It was after *To Have and Have Not*
that he married Bacall. Then three months down the line
was in a booth at Romanov's
downbeat, beaten, lost - asking Pete:
Any chance of picking up where we left off?

All that hype about three failed marriages,
then finding what he needed in Bacall -
baloney. The telegrams he sent her
were Pete's own words: *Miss you, love you,
miss you, hurry over - Bogie.*
It was no big deal.

*Whatever happens Pete, they can't say
we never lived* - was his favourite line.
Once in Salt Lake City, in the dry state of Utah,
some creep pointed to his glass of scotch and asked
Had he ever tried to stop? *Sure,* he said,
and it was the worst afternoon of my life.

PETE ON 'BOGART'S SECRET LIFE'

Hang on, there's more to it than that.
I'm not some sleazy footnote to his life
his prowess over women. Listen sister,
no one wipes their dirt on me. I chose
(and would again) to be his mistress.

I called time, while his third divorce
went through, knew once he got
unhitched, he'd grab like a drowning man
the first warm female body
he could find - and marry it.

Then the pattern would start over,
he'd come wheedling back
confessing to the latest
damned mistake he wanted out of.
I knew the truth, but still said yes.

A year before he died (unglued
he called it) I phoned long distance,
told him Walt and I were finally engaged
and were having champagne breakfast
in his favourite New York dive.

- You did it! he said, Put the booze
on my tab or I'll really be pissed off.
And Pete, he went on, I didn't want you to
and I did - you know?
I clicked my glass to the phone:

Here's to you, you ugly bastard.
- Now hang up, he laughed, I need some sleep,
it's 5am back here . . .
But there's more to it than that.
And always will be.

He'd always worry the morning after,
if he'd gotten too much
out of line the night before.
And how, I'd say, More
than you meant to.

He'd tug his ear the way he did on screen.
You'd swear to look at him
that that was it, the last time ever.
Save it, I'd say, I read you loud and clear.
C'mon, let's mingle.

THE SWING
after Fragonard

1

He saw her first on the upper deck,
that V-neck top, that A-line skirt.
They caught each other's eye repeatedly,
re-visualised their lives aligned.

With the white cliff's chorus ever closer,
he went ahead belowdecks, on stairs
that halfway, doubled-back on themselves
slid under the landing she now walked across

to take his arrow gaze and give it back,
stand pressed against the balustrade, as close
as she could to the thin, metal uprights
directly over him when he looked up.

2

So much for art. It's what went off
when brushes were set down,
the smock removed, that frames the act
says what it is to be alive.

Things won't move on, the image
unpossess the mind, until it's overlaid
debased of colour, meaning, purpose,
any virtuousity of line.

A portrait of the artist
as an over-rubbed balloon,
so static-charged he'd stick to ceilings,
gangways, walls

before he found the Gents amidships
to earth himself at lightning speed
into a cold urinal's
pouting mouth.

3

I bought the skirt especially, begged her
to please be *en plein air* beneath -
enjoy the ease of in and out,
then reach the swing in its hidden clearing.

A jagged bolt of naked branch
electrifies the scene. Her high-kick over me -
shoe flying off, my every watching leaf
arrhythmic in that flash of sun.

Again, again. And then again.
Until the world puts a finger to its lips,
draws curtains down: *Enough,*
this much and no more. No more now.

THE LOSS

Tomorrow they cinder Uncle Bill
with the minimum inconvenience.
10am Crematorium
cup of tea at No.51
if I cared to join them.

It wasn't him, these past few months,
swearing, making himself a nuisance
in the women's lounge. They swore one day
he tried to pull his dick clean off.
It's a release, says Flo.

Last time we met he stood looking,
anxious to get me right, had my hand
in his for ages, then just said *Aye*
and sat down again. Love holds on
like phlegm lodged in a sink.

It's waterfalls (or funerals) obsess me now -
describing them but meaning her -
a minor breakthrough at the time.
What would be happiness? - You can't lay a ghost
when the ghost won't talk to you.

Favourite colour? - Black
with just a hint of henna.
Smell? - Coconut shampoo.
Favourite taste? - Oh, what's it called,
on the tip of my toungue.

FOUR THINGS I LOVE ABOUT HER

One, her softness - only 5% of which is outwardly visible.
You and her, they'd say, Surely not. She's quartzite, toughened glass,
all tenderness would run straight off - is what they think.
But the one she chooses, he sees it all, even the void
this giving leaves in her, the void whose shape he is.

Two, her sexiness - which in all respects will be a perfect match to his.
You couldn't say which of them would be the figure, which the shadow.
Both give the other license to begin or be begun upon
at any point in the continuum. She fucks like angels would,
desiring what is most divine, spurring all nine heavens to a gallop.

Three, her defiance - which can be bristling, venomous - head thrown back,
a confident stride towards you. For she is, above all else, alive,
and demands what follows from that fact. Try palming second best on her -
a duff pint for instance, a flip word, a selfish act -
she'll march straight back, insist with a tough gaiety, you try again.

Four, her smile - which takes a high-cheeked, mannish face and the line
of a sometimes cruellish mouth, and makes every idol you've ever seen,
whoever on the screen is beautiful, less worth the looking at than her.
A smile whose sense is pure enclosure, the way ahead no longer linear,
but which says, at long last, after many false starts - you've arrived.

And this last thing, as coda - on her bed, making love, her above,
her eyes locked onto mine, and she's saying, and she's saying:
I love you I love you I love you I love you I love you
in time to every thrust and feint we make, and to that last half-moment
lost between the two. This a memory now, and the last to fade.

Yours, he said, was wonderfully apt,
slinking out together for a midnight walk:
Bee-at-ree-chee (whispered the Italian way)
its softness lingered on the dark, in quiet
filterings of rain. All night I saw us
twinned and twisting, braided to a heat
neither tiredness nor sleep could break -
only your disappearing footsteps on the stair.
And the morning up all innocence:
Oh what a dream I had. Life light as eggshell
in our hands - in the lift to the station,
in the faces of the couple, the man with the baby
in a free-fall sleep across his knee,
in our goodbye, the weekend over, and the game.

*

That's fine, she said, apart from that last line.
Fine in spirit, not as flesh. Tell them
how my short skirt looked, how I blushed
to see you stare. A tangerine and Trail-Pack nuts,
my choicest coy remarks were what I plied you with.
While you were no less devious - the good scout
well prepared in that room of whispers - condoms
and a candle ready lit! It burned for hours, for days.
Friends said I seemed a different me. I floated
wraith-like through the week, a vision
barely touching ground. But listen
it was not a dream. Have you forgotten this -
it wasn't Dante, Gabriel or Yves,
I wanted you as plain old Shady Jack.

Tilleul

*Can you love someone for fourteen years
without so much as kissing them or
touching them, just being in their presence
five days out of seven, till the ache
gets so much each summer (as clothing thins)
you want to turn away and disappear
not see their face again, their photograph
nor any note you made describing how they looked
or what they said or didn't say that time
you finally confessed your love, then quickly
switched the topic to the scent of lime trees
at the window, that unpronounceable
tisane the blossom makes,
its sedative effect supposedly.*

The Night Garden

Then the first bird calls and I
stop thinking about sleep and think
of the magnolia, the poise
of its cup-white flowers, the cool
perfume of its scent
as I draw its lips to mine.

But I must remember not
to take your hand, though I go to take it
many times, must remember
we are not lovers, and can never be
no matter how near sometimes
or unfantastical that seems.

So I stop thinking about sleep
or the scent of another life
on my lips, until a second bird
answering and calling to the first,
begins a synchrony we both could wait
forever for, and never hear.

Exposure Cravings

Blouse fastened a button lower than usual
so its plunge is the light of my gaze all day.
It can't go further but let's flirt the limits.

Exchanging photographs for instance,
that waxing curve of you exposed to full,
for any angle on me you might like:
a tide-me-over-to-the-next-time shot
I'm likely to hang onto forever.

Or movie clips we take ourselves,
to show our separate ways of saying
you and me together when we're not,
hoping no one downstairs hears what's
going off (unstoppably now)
as if at the touch of a button.

*

It's a *No*, of course. To underscore
the point you recount Sunday's lie-in,
Bob channel-hopping, finding Gary Rhodes,
Pork pies! cries Bob as he heads for the loo,
The guy's a fucking genius.
No doubt you laughed the way you're laughing now.
Perhaps it made you reach out with -
I do love you, when he's back beside
the toasty warmth of your T-shirt
or whatever you had on up to that point.

Bob's not allowed his pork pies now, you add
drawing your blouse wings shut, a hand spread wide
across your chest as if to say - I say this
to be kind. Don't hope. Don't dream. Don't even look.

His Latest Pitch

Here's the draft first chapter of a 'Boy Meets Girl'.
Let's write it together, at least be lovers on the page:

"That point in the do when the band's on song
and everyone's yabbering ten to the dozen, I wanted
to lean in and say it then. So when your mouth mouthed
What? my lips could bed your hair again, shout it
as the band stops dead. Each note, each breath
held on the line: *'If I could hold you now . . .'*
Eleven twenty nine you left, the Stratocaster
in a riff of spots turns green, then blue,
then one all-blinding dazzle of silver."

It's based on me, she hissed next day, *I couldn't possibly.*
That's fine, he says.
                    Who's kidding who? A smile is all
it takes to mire him in one more bad beginning.

Watching Anna Karenina

They spent the whole film, her left hand flirting
his right, running fingertips from underwrist
to palm and back again, over and over -
the lightest touch and all it stood for.

But when he said: *I want so much to kiss you*
her lips tightened, her head moved slightly
side to side, through two or three degrees,
so slight, he wasn't clear how sure she'd been
to have him focus on the scene at hand:
late sun, a snowy dacha fast-receding
out of view, dark woods beyond . . .

But their two hands would not be stopped
and went on making love as if nothing
had happened when everything had.

Before And After It Happened

This morning, I rinsed your cup out in the sink,
ran my fingers round the rim and down inside.

While it was happening all I could think was
seeing your head on my pillow, this
is what it is to have no wishes left.

So how will the kettle half an hour later
give the impression nothing has changed?

A Flint From Birley Gap

Here's a way to hold me, bring back the heat
we've raised together, with no one knowing
when or how - this flint: its night-face flecked
with nebulae, the whole Big Bang of us;
while its chalk-blank underside shows nothing
and keeps shtum. Who's to guess when we're both gone
what guided your kisses to mine, or the words it took
(my all-time best) to draw you to my bed?

Touch me - make me yours, my keepsake heart
at blood-heat in your pocket, in your palm.
Let it be eloquent on my behalf.
If it fails - throw it back into the sea,
let the next millenia perfect it.
Maybe then I'd have a chance with you.

Displacement

It's never either/or. What law says two
enduring loves can't co-exist? Now it's dark
by five, we meet on the short drive home
to quickly snatch a kiss, then fast on the first -
four more. One night should we just keep going?
A weekend in Sussex, three weeks in Cassis?
Sometimes it takes that vase of flowers,
a second timeless still-life in the hall,
to realise how vast in happiness
love is, how loving grows with every love
we have.
                    I left the porch light burning
just in case. Next day, you told how
half way home, you'd slowed, pulled over, grabbed
the phone to phone me. But then drove on.

                        *

The Tuscan night has fallen, plane trees lamplit
in the square, a shuttered room where she lies
sea-lulled, trace of salt still stiffening her hair
suncream in the crook of an arm.

For him, the smell of sea rain, blackened rocks.
Melvaig - bay of bent grasses. Soft rush and bog rush
flooring the roofless house in an unkempt croft
where he stares out across the Minch
as the Hebredies go down in light, cloud-flame
soused in darkness, steel blues to umber grey.

An unlit moon lifts southwards over Raasay
and the slate flat sea. He turns to leave
but cannot look away. The Tuscan night
has fallen; smell of sea rain, slate flat sea.

The Telling Look

He's a love. If folk say anything of me,
that's what I'd have them say. Someone I helped
with an application once, said as she left
the office, design problem solved:
I'm so happy I could give you a love.

No need for stars, we're in each other's arms
by simply sitting close, skin brushes skin
with every telling look. Our separateness
the two beats of a cuckoo's call, each part
distinct but inextricably conjoined
twin notes that can't exist without the other.

Whether you're in my arms again or not,
I'll stand beside this gorse-lit gateway
yesterday, tomorrow. And beyond.

The Man On The Bench

appears bent double, staring at the ground in front
like an old man, or a man trying to regain
his senses, but when a young woman tiptoes up
arms raised, a ballerina, and touches him
so lightly on the shoulder, then moves off swiftly,
he gets up, follows, suddenly lithe and fit
a young man, as young as she is, younger.

At that point you turn to say: *Tonight can't happen
I'm afraid. Would that spoil your day? You're sure?
Tomorrow then.* Then turn and go.
                                        Anger,
disappointment - yes, but something else, the urge
to pull away (though it's already much too late).
I sit on that same bench staring at the line of trees
then the dust and fag ends on the ground in front.

                         *

When you said Goodnight, and went to your own room,
dreams like a final, unloosed petal
fell from the bone-headed moon.
                                        Next day
our train raced estuaries, waves of ploughland
the colour of tile, trees the green of my eyes,
you said. By willing it to happen (why
didn't it last night?) a distant signal
turns to amber - the colour of the speckle
in yours. We slow, but not enough to stop
the world or put the moon back in its sky.

Remember the azalea, that yellow
lutea, and bending time and again
to its scent, grains of pollen dusting
the tip of your nose, then mine.

Accepting Winter for What It Is

Time, Einstein found, slows down in a wood
unlike elsewhere in the cosmos, light slows also
which does things to distance you wouldn't believe.
Mileva was his proof under the leaves.

The month when honeysuckle, no scent left
in its last flower, is finally exhausted, the wood becalmed.
Only birds jitter the rigging, stir the leaves.

Was it goldcrests or firecrests in the topmost branches?
Tiny brakes squeak-binding tiny wheels as you broke free.

*

Ridiculously hopeful or hopelessly dire,
here's the coming year in snowdrops at my door:
light-winged on good days; tight-lipped on bad.

You apologised ten minutes in, for being
non-orgasmic, said the prospect of our tryst
had made you "frisky" (twice) the night before,
a sure-fire guarantee our safe sex just got safer.
But hey, it was good to be close. What am I saying?
It was brilliancy itself. Good too, to be
reminded where allegiance has to lie.

Rydal Water

Just as, looking down from Nab Scar, hot and parched
from off the fells, to see it glittery below
and thinking how the best thing in the world
would be to slide into its depths - I thought how
yesterday as you were leaving, you seemed
cool and distant, eager to be gone.

Then wading in, the water brown not blue, chill
and weedy, silt stinking underfoot, a threadworm
on the surface, enough to kill off all desire
and make one gaze instead at the breeze-blown
fastness of Nab Scar - just so tomorrow
hearing what all weekend I dream you'd say,
you'll say it, and that second I'll seem cool
and distant, only half inclined to stay.

Dead Reckoning

I need time, she says (this justifies anything
she cares to name), *Let's leave it for a while . . .*
Those August evenings he searched out her car
left notes, sweet peas beneath the wiper blades;
last week she paid him back by not walking
the twenty yards it took to do the same.
He's a three year old that's close on fifty.
He's sly, mixed up and must be punished.
She gives him time to write out all these lines.

He killed a lamb once, pressed its head into a pool
until the bubbles stopped. Astonishing, how long
a weak, crow-blinded thing can cling to life.

Have it your way then. It's finished! The look
she gave him then - a fool might call it love.

                  *

This morning I slammed a sauntering pheasant down
half avoiding, half aiming for the kill. Half-penitent,
half glad. Though less assured in finishing the job
when, head half beaten off, it spiralled back to life
in one last bloodied stand.
                      Untied, the pheasant's heart
is thumbnail size, it's nub of muscle bloody
on my outstretched palm. All I've stalled or ended short
confronts with conscience now.
                      Time I took stock
of my evasions, find one last tryst-place
in the wood, in case it can come good between us.
Though one last day's embrace must end it soon.

Best not say a word about the fox cub
thrown aside for the flies, its fur still dawn-bright
still so new to the darkness of this world.

Ending It

She wanted the strength to end it.
Or for him to.

Their last act together -
to hold down the pillow on their love.

After five days - a text.
Soaring and terrible those lungfuls of hope.

*

We almost made it. That double room
was waiting in the courtyard B&B.
Instead you burn my notes, incinerate
confessions. The relief - to be spotless again,
all trace of what went on wiped clear.

Outside, lime blossom frenzies the tumult
of a million bees. This time last year, that was us -
uncontainable. How quickly lust exhausts
its oxygen. I lied to everyone including you,
to engineer an hour to ourselves.
Not just to fuck, as you supposed,
but let in light and air, admit the trees
whose time it was, hear once more the quick
jubilant shriek of the here-and-gone swift.

Leaving Present

How long can you love someone
without the hope of holding them again,
no future easement in their arms,
no light in the dunnock's song, no flag
on the stone folly flying.
                              Time to quit
give notice and finally move on.

For a leaving present when you go -
one kiss. And not the much-kissed air
beside their cheek, but a proper kiss
worth all those years of waiting.
Fifteen years, from the day you met to this,
and for whatever stays unfinished.
One kiss, a fifteen second kiss,
time it - it lasts forever.

LITTLE GREBE

Rocks turn tail as a scurry of moorhens.
Twigs flit the gap to the next bare tree
as a chitter of finches. The dabchick meanwhile
buoys to the top of the bluebrown river.
That knuckle of water, dive-alert,
re-liquifies as soon as look at you,
stays gone for good, while you stand mud-shoed
in a tangle of tree roots and longing,
so firmly untransmutable it hurts.

THE RESCUE DREAM

Upped bobbed the body. I ran to the edge
and hauled it ashore. Only a torso
the headless and limbless trunk of a man.
But with palm bracing palm I pumped at the heart
for all I was worth. Till a shock of water
shot from the neck. Another. Then more.
Then a pulse kicked in and limbs re-branched
and grasped at the stones. The head re-emerged.
Eyes came alive. And opened again into mine.

THE RUNNING STREAM

Half a lifetime spent
watching the river
journey through a single day.

Work. Then home again.
No time to know the river's flow:
without; within.

As light goes, love has nowhere
to settle. It hurts so much:
flowing on.

The day bled colour.
All things stopped. The river
kept the world's heart beating.

With the third star
the new day stars. Water wakes
as a field of moonlight.

Dawn poppies. Mist-floe
of crowsfoot. A dabchick
dolphins the flowery stream.

How few summers left now?
Twelve? Ten? Floods of light
on the morning river.

TWO BLACKBIRDS

in memory of Ann Atkinson

One Day

The blackbird is singing by the room you woke in;
same split oak whistling in the range at breakfast, though the air
outside is warm. The lake too. Remember wading in
it seemed forever, through the slatey shallows of the bay;
that wind-shored hike onto High Spy; the meal you served
that evening; an after-life of poems shared.

At the time, one day among many, replayable surely
as and when? The blackbird after all is back again
on the lilac, this time singing everyone to sleep
and you - with such an eagerness - into our waking.

Five Years On

At dawn a blackbird taps the bathroom window
raps itself at the bedroom window
to wake me surely. Which it does. Make me
remember as I walk the lake - the bay
coved round with oak and larch, sweetened gold
with gorse and wild azalea, where we
waded in that red-hot day, the bed so gradual
it took an age to get above our knees,
our thighs, to slip right in, up to our necks
so to speak; and glad of it, happy
we said *Yes, why not*; it felt so fine,
a windfall blessing every single time.

All such a long time ago now - but when
I reach down and touch it, the water's still warm.

LETTER FROM MAJORCA

1

You always said we should fall in love
with each other, it would solve everything,
the habitual mess our love lives were in.
Though for years we had the next best thing -
to lay together, say whatever came to mind
stuff we'd never tell another soul, that sometimes
we weren't proud of, that brought again
that sense of failure in our lives. But not just then.
Then was intimacy way beyond the sexual,
not easy to explain or comprehend
what we neither of us found elsewhere but curled
together over-wintering an hour in each other's warmth.
Why doesn't everyone do this? you said.
What better way to have our truth more simply told
than by legs and arms and body heat alone.

2

We laughed about the one time we made love,
how instantly forgettable it was. So much so
we remembered different occasions, in separate locations
entirely. And no amount of prompting would double our tally.
What sort of bargain had we struck? Shielding the other
from what embarassment, humiliation? As if
we'd been together all our lives and knew
the other's vulnerabilities and restlessness.
Those last two years it came together,
your writing found its rightful stage
and you - a matching confidence, elan.
You stood before us and all were dazzled.

3

So uncharacteristic that initial forgetfulness,
confusion over dates and times. Your daughter phoning:
Where are you? Your grandson's party's underway.
Should I bake? you say. *No mum, just come round . . .*
I turned up one day as arranged, winter jasmine
at your door, to find you unprepared. *Is it that time?*
you asked, half-concealing what you'd not foreseen . . .
A brain scan found the tumour and you Facebooked
its name and grade. We found out for ourselves
what that implied. Knew at once it wasn't good.

4

They brought you home to die. 'Very scared'
is how one text ended . . . Loved ones. Friends.
Your chair. That rug. The vase of larkspur
on the hallway stand. All savoured, wept for, put aside.
It came down to favourite music by the bed. Your hand
being held. How could that ever be enough?

5

This teak-dark acorn on the hill by Valldemossa -
your eyes had the same deep lustre. I can't
walk by without a second look, or on without it.
Evergreen oaks. Instant summer when the sun appears
and times that rope-thin cypress through its hours.
We meant to winter here one year, Chopin and Sand,
all the time in the world, and a notebook to fill
on how the locals in their knee-length jackets
think this middling spring warmth winter,
though bougainvillea catwalks every wall-top;
how dark the seedpods of the carob - fallen sickles
gone to waste; how pink, that first blossom
(almond? prunus?) brightening a little more each day
the January wind.

CONCERT FOR ANN

The cello wept
but wept in a good way

moved between a dark place
and a sunlit edge

holding and letting you go
never letting you go.

SLUGS

It must have seemed like heaven after weeks of drought.
Out they came from the douching shrubberies
over the skidpan path to the glutted lawn.

I counted twenty in the rabbit's run, a dozen
feasting on his concentrate, draped like gumshields round his bowl,
a four-inch keel back in his water dish.

The rabbit looked at me, I looked at him. Then filled
a bucket from the butt, grabbed the fattest, longest, blackest
slug by its bunching midriff and dunked it in.

Unsuckered more from the sides of the hutch, from the run's
grey sheeting, plipped them to the bottom of the pail.
But as the last were finally un-polyped, the first

were leeching back up the sides of the bucket,
out from the water, up to the rim . . .
Have you seen how slugs make love? Take two Great Greys,

some seven inches long. They hoop into a dough-nut shape
lick each other for two hours plus, before lowering themselves
from a branch or wall on a phlegm-thick cord of slime.

Once there - hermaphrodites - they both unroll a two inch
penis, both swap sperm. Then it's back up the cord
to lay their eggs, scoffing the ladder as they go . . .

Anyway, I flip them under once again, take the whole lot
to the churchyard and - giving God his creatures back -
sluice them out into a heap, their undersides all whites and yellows,

like someone's innards, or a shellfish dinner someone hadn't
managed to keep down, and which now starts moving
crawling off in all directions with far from sluggish zest.

The rabbit looked at me, I looked at him. Then set him free.
But all he does is find his own spot on the lawn
and lords it there, immovable. Unquestionably fine by me.

HOOPOE

Or half of one - the back half
diving away. Hoopoe! we hollered
clocking zebra-banded secondaries,
white mid-band on a black fanned tail,

but not the clinching ruddy crest -
a swept-back quiff or feathered head-dress
when upraised - nor too
the Samarai-slender, down-curved bill.

The group behind saw nothing
but were mad to, everytime a jay
or thrush broke cover. So many
false alarms it seemed neater in the end

to accuse ourselves of wishful thinking.
Had we really seen so rare a thing?
An exotic more at home in Gauguin's
art than on our walk. Ghost bird

at a sleeper's head, rune-word
for so wrapt and wondrous a revelation
it lingers there in bands of shuttered sunlight
when we wake. Perhaps a glimpse

is all we get, are ever meant
to get, the wonderment evasive
to the end - as the day, the hour, the minute
turns aside, and dives beyond.

RESTING KINGFISHER

An individual life is of no consequence.
The resting kingfisher, abridged to a glow
in the wavering stream is a comma of bronze,
viridian, bright alchemical blue,
already its own abbreviated rainbow.

My fibreglass rod will outlast me.
That time a kingfisher settled on its tip
while the river held me fixed, won't come again.
She - for I'd like to think it was a she
who deftly, lightly stretched out a hand -
paused there a moment to show me the way.

PRICKS

Eric Gill's icebreaker with any new female he met
was to offer a ruler and ask if she'd measure him
flaccid and erect - the light of God's glory
always to hand beneath his artisan smock.
What a prat! I thought. Then remembered

I'd sent a polaroid of mine to a couple of women
I was crazy for, thinking it would ease things up
in the bedroom department, with less disappointment too
since apologies for being on the shy side
of average accompanied the shot. Mags, bless her

sent back by return some six by fours, all
body paint and shadow. Ideal, as calling cards go.
On our first night, it could have been the host
she was taking so keen was she, calling it -
though I took this with a dose of salt - divine.

Down-siftings of may where water crowfoot
sheets the leafy, slowworm river, and ramsons'
starry linen overspreads the wood.

It's gone beyond our choosing love or friendship,
our kisses, those long purples in the grass, see to that.
Is it lunch on the spread cloth of the ground
or something more? Either course has its regrets.
But all there is, is what your eyes are saying.

The Wye's blue shimmer tattoo
on the cliff's white shoulder; white
ribboning dark water under a wind-ruffled swan;
all the multitudinous shiftings of the world
come to rest on our skins' white stillness and pause.
Kiss again. Again, again.

                              *

That kiss changed everything, the moment
of surrender there already (your reflection
quizzing mine quizzing yours by the bed-dents
in the carpet, in the mirror on the wall)
whether or not we ever kiss again.
I can't not say *I love you* every other word,
not stop each step we take to kiss once more.
And each more urgent than the first,
reaching beyond what kisses ought to know
of who we are and what we want.
But the ache when they stop - far worse.

You and I - a bowl of kisses no amount
of kissing ever fills. Now I can't wait
to give you this - another way of kissing.

THE HIDE

(What's the glimpse of an otter,
the sweetest, vivace show
a chiffchaff offers, to the touch
of an arm or brow?)

We couldn't believe our luck
entering the hide, and side
by side up-swung the shutter
on what lay before us -

kingfisher, widgeon, a tow-line
of goose-hauled goslings -

when first one twitcher, then
another, gathered up
their things, swung shutters to,
and silently as through

a darkened church, on
tiptoe left us to it.

IMMERSION

poem with a phrase of Katherine Mansfield

Now I'm down to shorts and lotion, do I want
to go in? A cold cloud crosses the lake.
Round the bay the gorse has fizzled out. The few
bright yellows left show how much has been lost.
If they were roses they'd be tossed away.

But here's the *puff of gold-dust* under our
wading steps: two damselflies, lit cobalt rods
hitched head to tail in tandem flight, skim the rushes
refuelling the world with damselflies. And peel away
spent petals, a swelling gorse-seed's set to show.

Once in, I'm fine. It's now I always whisper
(to myself as much as you, love): *Once in,
I never want out again. Ever.* At which,
you always smile and bring me further in.

THE DIPPER THING

So thoroughly itself
with its stretch of river

it's no surprise when its eye
in its delicate eye-ring
of white mascara
shows with each blink

an eyelid as white
as the lid of an ice-pool
dusted with snow, nor
when it opens again

that the quick colley eye
of the river stares back.

*

And being the river's
for as long as it has,
its song's a blackbird's
rescored for the water

with phrasings and pitch
a match for the torrent
that pours by its feet
and white-riffle breast,

this rib of the river
reissues itself
as a flurry of notes
shakes snow from its back.

*

When a small white
fish dashed down on
rock three times four
times, is this time
swallowed

the dipper
does the dipper
thing, sits white-bibbed
on his white-bibbed rock

takes such small sips
of the hurrying stream.

BALLERINA WARBLER

Identified by its effortless upward spring
the way it tiptoes air, taking invisible flies
over the meadow's open cistern.

Pirouetting done, another flits in from the wings
same centre-stage routine. Then more appear
a corps of matching talents

five, six, eight at least
without my glasses. Without my field guide,
unforgettable.

MIRÓ'S STAR

He put an x on the postcard to his mother
to show their room on the hotel's seaward side.
Pilar, his bride of three days, signs it too: *Happy
Felicitations*. No word though of the bay's
bright setting or the new light of expression
in her eyes, that lifts them night-wings beating hard
through the pine-appliquéd dark.
                                        He makes the *star*
from that point on his all-time favourite mark,
up there with moon and nightingale, vagina, rose
and phallus. *Everything*, the postcard ends,
No less than unforgettable.

THE CROSSING

To cross and reach the road ahead
we had to put our swim suits on and swim out
to where the waves got more threatening,
the undertow stronger. We had to launch ourselves
upwards as each surge approached us. We were
getting exhausted when there in mid-Channel
the sea-bed rose nearer, and we saw on the bottom -
rail-lines and gantries, and under the water
an on-rushing train, which having swept by us,
we dived for some coaches submerged in a siding.
You beckoned me closer, I watched your lips open:
If the train's not running I'm going no further.
Each silver-foiled word wobbled huge to the surface,
then up to the stratosphere, out into outnesses
no one has reached yet. But it was. And we did.

ANNABEL AND *THE GHOST ORCHID*

Driving back from the reading, you were inspired.
You rooted through the glove-box for your tape of the book.
We began where it happened to be,
with Baucis & Philemon, the inseparables,
and played it through to the finish, till we were there
at the road-end to drop me off, and say Goodnight.

Now past midnight, I take the book and read backwards
from the last page, each poem an echo of where we were
when you turned from your driving to look at me
and repeat, elated, each felicity out loud,
poem after poem back to where we started, to where the journey
could begin again, image by image, look by look.

AUGUST
for Michael Longley

Inside the garden
white blossom on white blossom:
the poet writing.

WINTER HELIOTROPE

A friend announced this week that a tumour on the optic nerve
behind her eye, means she'll be blind before the summer comes,
but added, since flowers are her special thing, that come July
she'll be looking to the scents outside for all that colour.

In the lane by her door, though it was winter, the hedgerow
colourless and dead, I had the sudden, vanilla scent
of honeysuckle, roses - but could see nothing anywhere in flower,
except for one low growing thing you wouldn't look at twice.

I guessed at burdock and was months adrift - it wouldn't bloom
until July and had no scent, unlike this flower which had me
on my knees, closing my eyes to breathe more deeply
on its tiny, unkempt tassels of inconsequential pink.

Like the poet Akahito who, twelve centuries before,
coming light-heartedly to pick violets, found a fragrance there
he fell so far towards, he found it difficult to leave,
so didn't leave, but slept all night beside that field.

WAY BEYOND THE RIVER NOW

The thinnest smoke-strand lifts
from a pollinating nettle, tricks away
to nothing, stokes my greedy gaze for more,
when once should be enough, but never was.

Where do years of passion leave us?
A decade's moment gamed and gone.

Yellow hawkbit, starry mayweed
drift out the field to a line of poplars
their breezy static overhead, louder
and deeper the nearer we get.

PLATE TECTONICS
for Linda Rice

You're moving away from me.
Day after day we're further apart.
Such sly, inexorable increments.
I never realised. You never realised.

Look east now from your Minnesota garden.
I'm on Black Knoll, Long Mynd, face on
to a keen westerly. Wave to me Linda.
Wave to me, please. Before it's too late.

STARGAZER

If the sun was a basketball sized with gold
then forty metres down the road, balanced
on a silver pin, a seed-pearl painted blue -
would be the earth. A hand's width away, little more
than a fattened pinhead on its own small pin -
the totally inconsequential moon.

At that scale, I'd have to get in my car
(and the next four cars I'd ever own
for one car wouldn't last that far) and drive flat out
at eighty, day and night for one whole year,
to reach the twin paper lanterns
of Alpha Centauri. That's how close the next star is.

*

Lilies milk the darkness with their scent. You should
be here with me tonight scaling the universe.
Keep your eyes to the path not me, you'd say
as we saunter by planets, upending gravities
to race upstairs in a whirl of mutuality, reach
from zero to infinity in three seconds flat.

Instead of which, we sat there on our last night
worlds apart. Words, no matter how appointed
always fall short of what our lips would say.
Enclosed are photographs. Send some of you.
The one I took is distant, indistinct,
too far away to see your eyes.

THE APPLE GARDEN

Since we cannot meet, my gaze goes to the blossom
its countless ways of blending carmine into white
and laying both against a complementing green;
but choose however many stems I lean towards
when I inhale there's only one scent there for me.

*

I didn't tell you this but when you left
I went into your room and in the bathroom bin
found a drum of body powder with enough left in
when I turned the four holes in the top and tapped it out
against my skin to sense the touch of you again.

*

It's more than a taking off of make-up
when the last petal falls, it's a turning inwards
or a facing away - becoming something no one
sees or thinks twice about: it's just a tree
that's all, perhaps that's all it ever was.

*

I write to ask: *Is everything provisional?*
You write that blossom is, *but not good friendship*
or lovers who are friends. It's months until we meet again
and the tree reappears, blushed and glorious
under its apples. All it takes is our belief.

WOODHUISH

What is there about March, I asked,
Why you love it so much? What she said
said as much about herself: *The trees,*
she said, *are at their most beautiful!*

I stared as if for the first time, at wind-bared oak,
skylined ash. *See,* she said, *the added*
definition each twig has. And it's not
the light, but the latency light brings.

Like candles at our bedside hint
at what comes next, and precisely how
it feels. And the thrill of that as strong
or stronger, than the thing itself.

She stopped. And I saw the way
when we make love, she stops mid-breath
to stare transfixed, as if at trees
whose every leaf of every leaf is suddenly

in one quick moment of release, released
and shaken out. *It's then,* I said,
saying as much about myself, *Then*
you are at your most beautiful.

THE INVISIBLE MAN

Will there be time to read? you ask, *That fat novel -*
Vikram Seth's! I'll bring that along.
I'll bring it too, I say, *With a copy under both feet*
you'll be the perfect height against the bedroom wall.

At which point Liz and Phil appear - half glance, half smile
(the way you do, entering a cafe
and the table by the door looks up) - then instantly
walk straight on past, without a word.

It's your blue jumper, you tell me, *It blends too well*
with the décor. That, or seeing me with you.
Perhaps they knew what you wanted most at that moment
was invisibility. And they were kind.

I crashed a party once like that, I tell you this
to fill the silence, *My face, head, hands, completely bandaged,*
a thin slit for my eyes. I told the Pirates, Vampires,
Vicars, I was Ray Milland.

With no face to lose I could afford for once to be myself.
Loud, chancy, invulnerable. As amusing or abusive
as I pleased. A hit at last. Not the quiet lad
they'd known for years, who was at base, a nobody.

Invisibility had finally made a man of me.
The trouble was, I couldn't move my jaw to eat.
And who would fancy anyone with no skin,
however clean the wrappings.

I tore them off except from round my head,
dolloped ketchup on a frontal lobe,
rejoined the ranks of the Walking Wounded -
withdrawn, defeated, more invisible than ever. . .

Here you lean over, make as if I can't be seen, pat
your way across my features to touch-locate two lips.
Better grab your crutch, soldier! you say,
You'll need it next weekend. After all that reading.

DOLCE VITA

The Tower

Siesta time in Vezio
but the hawks on their tethers
in the shade of the castle
stayed watchful,

eight flights up, we bent over battlements
to the cardinal points: three giving onto
the sun-shocked lake, one to a huddle
of roofs below,

which was where I came up behind you
my gentle pressure matched
by pressure of your own: no one around
why shouldn't we there and then?

but something in the sunlight held us back,
only in the cellar's
furthest, darkest room
did the right moment come:

the tower, the vaulted door at its root
and the peregrine
stretching out a talon in the heat
extending one miraculous wing.

At Table

That night, in Henry Fielding mode,
a citronella candle on the balcony
the lights of Varenna necklacing the lake,
we do the *Tom Jones* thing
of best course last,

as the sweet plate's pushed aside
your skirt's pulled back:
what's sundaed there
brings me to my knees
to mouth a breathless grace,

which opened shutters on the floor above -
Basta, basta - to be as swiftly shut:
you simply pulled me closer
to the wall, pushed the table
out of harm's way: on cue,

the last Bellagio ferry broke in with a hoot
and crash of gangways pulled ashore:
which might have been a metaphor
for getting up to leave, not slipping off
as we did then, to bed.

The Exciting Bit

I was born to fuck you: said, in thrall
to the seed-pearl spur of you,
the milky blindness of its eye;

while you, still book in hand, plough on
towards the plot's denouement:
Go on then, get on with it.

THE MIRACLE

Loving as we were, the place and the B&B
what took the edge off slightly was the tidemark
of plastic, high and dry on sand and marram grass
in every cove and quiet inlet that we tried.

We wanted someone to say Enough: bring litter louts
and plastic industry execs plover-tumbling
from the sky to out-scurry the dunlin
in a wand-like transformation of the shore.

We wanted someone to stretch a magic arm
around the U-bend in the loo for the Dutch cap
that had slipped its berth in error and been flushed away,

and have it proudly buffed and gleaming
on the edge of the bath when we got back in
from the miracle outside, still wanting more.

INTIMACY

I can't do this, you said, gripping the sides
of the bath. Then suddenly: *Oh, it's coming!*
First drops and flickers, a sprinkling warmth
whose touch stirs and thickens me. More flow,
more reach, an affusion now
annointing belly, chest, almost the cup
of my neck, before falling shy again.

I can't believe I've done that, you said.
Nor the delight it gave, the unexpected
sense of giving and admitting of the other.
All we go on to be from here - is here,
was how you kissed me afterwards, how I
kissed you: two thirstlings at the font
of springs and rivers, soaked and newly blessed.

SOURCE OF THE WORLD

You rise from the bath
and cease being Marte;
it's Courbet not Bonnard
who kneels by the fire
to open your legs.

In the video clip
I play over and over,
my finger comes forward
shaking and weightless -
a leaf to the flame.

BILBERRY MOSS

Remember - bivouacked
on our bed of heather
your arm in my arm
my fingers your fingers
the dark of the solstice
swinging above us
a lift and a lightness
we'd never have dreamt of
if we tried - that skylark
climbing the darkness
to sing at the stars.

BEING ALIVE

Convinced every minute of the thirty years following,
that what killed him will, as night swallows day, take me too,

this morning I reached the age my father reached the day he died
to find myself still here, still fit, in apparent good health,

no signs I can't - touch wood, touch all in sight - go on savouring
for some time yet a glass of Shiraz with my evening meal -

tonight, a dish of rainbow trout, courgette and Jersey Royals;
or sip a nightcap to the newly demobbed moon on Haddon Hill;

or best of all - the sun tomorrow morning stealing in
through the open summerhouse door to sit over me

take my whole naked body in its mouth.

LATE MATINÉE

In a matter of moments
white flame of blackthorn
is catching the pulse, red kites
lift from the hills' blue wings.

So what if I'm not
what I was at forty
or fifty? The curtain's up
and somehow rising yet.

Soaring light proves
every skylark brightly weightless,
the high-up way it feels in love.
The stage a thousand suns

that only blossom
now our play's begun.

KATSURA TREE

There! Caramelised sugar on the woodland air.
We turned left not right on the Acer Trail
and missed first time those scent-filled yellows
and smokey pinks, the sweetness draining down
the breakup of each heart-shaped leaf.

You can taste the drift things take from here.
If only all decay could take the air that way.
This tree's the place we should make love beside,
hoping we'll never not be together,
the here and hereafter one breath apart.

FENNEL GRATIN

Our favourite dish hot from the grill. Tonight extra rich, its blend
of Gruyère, pesto, cream, melding perfectly the aniseedy fennel.
But what brought past betrayals bubbling up? So you, I, we
go over it again: *How could I? And why? Why? Why?*
till enough's enough, and a hand - yours, mine it makes no difference -
      reaches out and sets us back on course.

Remember how we met, when you first opened the door to me
in those tight white slacks, then turned your back, reached down
to pick up something from the floor. You swear you weren't that blatant
showcasing yourself like that, but looking back you had a catch
to hook, a dish to fry, and I got lucky - the barb went deep,
      then deeper each new time.

So the mouthful after - the fifth, fiftieth or fifteen hundredth
it makes no difference, our appetite's the same, the taste as silken -
that mouthful feels if anything more more-ish now, more who
we really are for all those countless times together, setting to
with thanks and a still indecent relish, mopping clean
      our plates, the dish, our fingers.

THE PRESENT

You couldn't make it up,
a midday nightingale
in trees below Aust Cliff,
his amplified clarity
unmistakeable
on the swooshing-by
backing of the M48.

Move left a tad, you said,
And forward.
Which put me closer the cleat
at the wharf's edge, my feet
where his were in '66
when Feinstein, Nikon poised, said:
Bob - towards me now.

The 'Judas' Tour
when Folk plugged into Rock.
The year I brought his EP home
'Dylan' the one word cover,
four heart-blowing songs
that closed my childhood
bridged me to another land.

Corrina, Corrina,
Gal, where you been so long.
Fifty four years on, that song
still pauses me to listen.
My own Corrina listens too.
But look around - it's hard
to see things as they were.

All the traffic's overhead.
Ferry signs and ticket office gone,
the jetty's ribcage swamped in reeds,
the Severn Princess banked in rust
on the Chepstow side.
And just about my whole life
played out too.

Everything gone west
except that cleat,
these sandstone slabs,
this boundless singing.
They alone have seen out
every minute every day
and stayed unchanged.

Then one last wonder -
a pair of Bar-Headed Geese
from the Himalayas,
with no cause to be here
grazing the saltings
seemingly content
with the world as it is.

The present keeps coming
whilever we listen.
Time unbettered
no matter the effort
or hopes put in. Love
the singing, love the songs,
love hearing them together.

WHAT I KNOW OF MIRAMAR

Pines set just so on the zigzags down
to the headland with its one sea eye,
glitterstars exploding soundlessly across a bay
whose blue seems neoned from within.

Who couldn't love this place: belvederes,
the rock-hewn boathouse, the jetty where a woman
stands naked, wringing out her hair, placing an arm
round her partner's (clothed) shoulder.
Wet strands fall forwards as they lean at the edge,
touch-stroke the side of his face. All the sighs
he's made in love or hope of love, the sea
must quicken with them now at her smile,
her slim brown body beside him . . .

And as though that moment stayed,
when they'd packed their things and left
and we took their place on the catwalk jetty,
you stripped off too, stood looking down
into that jewel-box sea, whose thousand shifting lights
beat on and off for me now.
Though never sure I love enough - too restless,
too ready to risk everything for what's already won,
I ask: *What's left to love in me?*

Your arm finds my shoulder, your lips my face:
Whatever makes love stronger, is your answer . . .

I climb the headland, to its topmost point,
gaze on sea, those pines, the road that led us here,
guided your kisses to mine, and which today for once
does not lead elsewhere. Leaning out to gaze below,
I see you cat-stretched on a towel in the blaze.
Your eyes must be closed but I wave nonetheless.
Stand and wave to every single thing.

ACKNOWLEDGEMENTS

I would like to thank the editors of the following publications in which some of these poems first appeared: *Antiphon; Arvon Journal; Blithe Spirit; Giant Steps; HQ Poetry Magazine; Lancaster Literature Festival Poetry Competition Anthologies; Northwords; Observer; Other Poetry; Poetry Ireland Review; Poetry London; Poetry Review; Poetry Wales; Rialto; Sheaf; Smiths Knoll; Staple; The Echo Room; The North; The Red Wheelbarrow; The Yellow Nib.*

'Plate Tectonics' appeared in *Ripening Cherries, An Anthology of Haiku, Tanka & Haibun,* published by Offa's Press (2019).

'Bogart's Secret Life', 'Four Things I Love About Her', 'Pillow Book', and 'The Invisible Man' were part of a sequence which won the Tom Roder Memorial Prize for Poetry, Sheffield University.

A number of the poems appeared in two self-published, limited edition pamphlets: *The Night Garden* (2013) and *Newdelight* (2017).

I have drawn on information in *Bogie and Me* by Verita Thompson published by WH Allen for the two poems: 'Bogart's Secret Life' and 'Pete on Bogart's Secret Life'.

Lastly, I would like to acknowledge my gratitude for Fellowships in Creative Writing at Hawthornden Castle, Scotland; Fondation Ledig-Rowohlt, Lavigny, Switzerland and The Helene Wurlitzer Foundation, Taos, New Mexico, where many of these poems were written. Thanks too, to Ray Russell of Tartarus Press for his help and encouragement.

PREVIOUS PUBLICATIONS

The Imbolc Bride (Littlewood Arc 1992)
Bursting The Clouds (Cape 1998)
Hokusai's Passion (pamphlet Offa's Press 2020)

BIOGRAPHY

John Sewell was born in South Yorkshire and educated in Scotland. Unable to choose between studying Art or English, he chose Architecture instead, (winning in his first year the Strathclyde University Poetry Competition and co-producing a pamphlet of Eliot-influenced poems riskily entitled: *Babel*).

After working in an architect's office in Sheffield, he realised William Carlos Williams meant more to him than Le Corbusier. Thereafter, he combined writing with doctoring buildings for the Peak District National Park.

He has two previous collections: *The Imbolc Bride* (Littlewood Arc) 1992 and *Bursting The Clouds* (Cape) 1998, and was co-author (with three others) of *The Blue Bang Theory* (Redbeck) 1997 - a collection of contemporary nature poetry. A pamphlet - *Hokusai's Passion: 36 Glimpses of Skiddaw* was published by Offa's Press in 2020. His poems have been on radio and appeared in various publications, including *Cambridge Encyclopedia of the English Language; Oxford Poetry Books for Juniors;* and *Poetry Book Society Anthologies*. He was featured in Poetry Review's *New British Poets II*.

Prizes include being a finalist in the Arvon International Poetry Competition, winner of the Sheffield Thursday Poetry Competition and three times winner of the York Open Poetry Competition.

He has been awarded a Writers Bursary, various Fellowships in the UK and abroad and was active for many years with the Arvon Foundation, both on the Council of Management and the Management Committee for Lumb Bank. He currently lives in South Shropshire and is a member of the Border Poets writing group.

ENDORSEMENTS

For Woods River Road:
These are fine poems about landscape, the weight of the word, the sensuous essence of things, the inevitable making of love. Images are tactile, colourful, a kingfisher glimpsed on on a fishing rod, hawks on their tethers, a midday nightingale. There are touches of sharp wit, of tenderness, of loss, of the complexity of love. Read these poems. Listen to those grasses bending in the wind.   Pauline Stainer

For The Imbolc Bride:
Sewell distills incident into its strongest elements, leaving the impression of an insight etched on steel, something felt and said with vivid finality. He's the real thing.   Anne Stevenson

He has an instinctive ability to use language in a very musical and original way.   Gillian Clarke

The language is original and strong. Yet his voice is tender. John Sewell writes beautifully. I shall read this collection again and again.   Iron Review

The Imbolc Bride is wonderfully fresh. The invocation of Celtic winter festivals lends this volume a dark resonance.   Time Out

For Bursting The Clouds:
Bursting The Clouds represents a bold development of the talent shown in Sewell's promising and very different first book.   Sunday Times

A gifted observer of the natural world.   Carol Rumens (Independent)

John Sewell knows how to ambush his readers. This funny, seductive, secretive little poem [The Response] is one of the gems of Bursting The Clouds. The poems explore marriage, lust, the end of marriage and a cold pastoral that was parallel to them and will outlive them.

Helen Dunmore (Observer)

I consider him to be a poet of great integrity, lyrical power and profundity.

Robin Robertson